How the ROCK CYCLE Works

Bethany Bryan

The Rosen Publishing Group's
PowerKids Press™
New York

Published in 2009 by The Rosen Publishing Group, Inc.
29 East 21st Street, New York, NY 10010

Book Design: Michael J. Flynn

Photo Credits: Cover © Halldor Eiriksson/Shutterstock; pp. 3–20 (background), 22–28 (background), 30–32 (background) © George Nazmi Bebawi/Shutterstock; p. 4 (stream) © Wong Yu Liang/Shutterstock; p. 5 (mountains) © Mike Norton/Shutterstock; p. 5 (street) © ppl/Shutterstock; p. 6 (gold nugget) © Diego Barucco/Shutterstock; p. 6 (topaz, amethyst) © Vasiliy Koval/Shutterstock; p. 7 (coal) © Daniel G. Mata/Shutterstock; p. 9 (Earth) © Andrea Danti/Shutterstock; pp. 10–11 (volcano) © juliengrondin/Shutterstock; pp. 12 (granite), 16 (strata), 18 (sandstone), 23 (shale, slate, mica schist), 30 (igneous rock, sedimentary rock) © Visuals Unlimited/Corbis; p. 13 (counter) © Chris Rodenberg Photography/Shutterstock; p. 14 (lava skylight) © Amy Nichole Harris/Shutterstock; p. 15 (basalt vase) © Sergey Khachatryan/Shutterstock; p. 17 (river mouth) © Galen Rowell/Corbis; p. 19 (fossil in limestone) © TimBPhotography/Shutterstock; pp. 20 (gneiss), 30 (metamorphic rock) © David Woods/Shutterstock; p. 21 © Paul C. Pet/zefa/Corbis; p. 22 (meteorite) © Sanford/Agliolo/Corbis; p. 22 (fulgurite) http://upload.wikimedia.org/wikipedia/commons/5/5b/Fulgurite1.jpg; p. 23 (clay) http://upload.wikimedia.org/wikipedia/commons/2/2c/Clay-ss-2005.jpg; p. 23 (phyllite) http://upload.wikimedia.org/wikipedia/commons/f/fe/PhylliteUSGOV.jpg; p. 25 (Earth) © Vladislav Gurfinkel/Shutterstock; p. 26 (volcano) © Jim Sugar/Corbis; p. 26 (girl eating spinach) © Phil Date/Shutterstock; p. 28 (boys looking at crystal) © Jutta Klee/Corbis; p. 29 © John Hoffman/Shutterstock; p. 30 (magma) © Charles Taylor/Shutterstock; p. 30 (sediment) © Photodisc.

Library of Congress Cataloging-in-Publication Data

Bryan, Bethany.
  How the rock cycle works / Bethany Bryan.
       p. cm. — (Real life readers)
  Includes index.
  ISBN: 978-1-4358-0151-6
  6-pack ISBN: 978-1-4358-0152-3
  ISBN 978-1-4358-2984-8 (library binding)
  1. Petrology—Juvenile literature. 2. Geochemical cycles—Juvenile literature. I. Title.
  QE432.2.B78 2009
  552—dc22

                              2008037610

Manufactured in the United States of America

Contents

Rocks Are Everywhere

Everywhere you go, there are rocks all around. Sidewalks are made of rocks. Many buildings you see are made of rocks in some form. Rocks can be almost any size. If you visit the Rocky Mountains in Colorado, you're actually visiting a group of huge rocks that formed millions of years ago. If you go to the beach and walk around on the sand, you're stepping on tiny bits of rock. Earth itself is an enormous ball of rock measuring almost 8,000 miles (12,900 km) across!

Rocks can be many different colors and sizes. They might feel rough or smooth. They might fall apart in your hand or be so hard that you can't

These are just a few of the places where you can find rocks on Earth. Where else can you see rocks in your world?

break them, even with a hammer. A rock's properties are determined by its composition, or what it's made from. Let's take a closer look at the rock **cycle** and learn how rocks are made.

topaz

amethyst

gold

Making and Breaking Rocks

Rocks are made up of tiny pieces of matter called minerals. Minerals are nonliving solids made out of more basic matter called elements. Elements—such as oxygen, carbon, and gold—are the **materials** that make up our world. Because there are so many different kinds of elements, there are many different kinds of minerals. Some minerals are made up of a single element, such as gold. Others are made up of two or more elements.

There are over 2,000 different types of minerals on Earth. When minerals come together under great pressure or heat, rocks form. This process might take a few minutes, or it might take millions of years. Rocks can contain any number of minerals. Therefore, there are many different types of rocks. To help organize the different kinds of rocks, scientists have separated them into three general groups: igneous rocks, sedimentary rocks, and metamorphic rocks.

You might think that after a rock forms, it stays where it is until someone digs it up. However, the formation of a rock is just the beginning.

Page 6 shows several common minerals. Coal, shown here, is a mineral that is made mostly of carbon.

A Look Inside Earth

Rocks continue to change, grow in size, break down into smaller pieces, and re-form because of constant forces such as heat and pressure. Water, wind, and chemical **erosion** also affect the formation of rocks. These changes are part of a never-ending process called the "rock cycle." But to fully understand the rock cycle, we need to take a closer look at Earth itself and the rocks that shape it.

If you could cut the Earth in half, you would see it's made of many layers. At the very center lies the inner core. The inner core is an extremely hot, solid ball made of the metals iron and nickel. The outer core is made of iron, nickel, and possibly the elements sulfur and oxygen. The outer core is **molten** due to the heat of the inner core. So why is the inner core solid? It's because the pressure is so great at that depth.

Around the outer core is Earth's thickest layer, called the mantle. The mantle is made mostly of very hot, solid rock, but it also contains melted rock called **magma**.

The surface of Earth is called the crust. The crust is made up of enormous slabs of solid rock called plates that actually float on top of the

As you can see from the picture on page 9, the crust is Earth's thinnest layer.

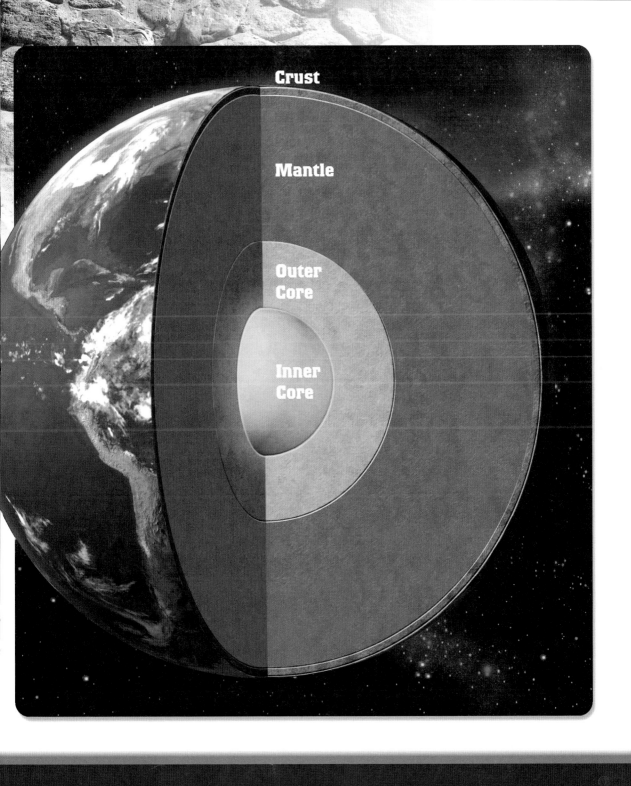

outer mantle. Fourteen large and many smaller plates make up Earth's crust. Because the plates are floating, they move and rub against one another. Where two plates come together, you can see the rock cycle at work!

Sometimes one plate crashes into another plate, or two plates pull away from each other. The edges of plates close together might rub against each other as the plates slide in different directions. Wherever any of these events occur, heat and pressure are generated. Where there is heat and pressure, rocks form.

Sometimes magma squeezes up to Earth's surface through gaps between plates. We see this when a volcano erupts. When magma cools, igneous rocks form. Let's look at them more closely.

	inner core	outer core	mantle	crust
average thickness	1,600 miles (2,600 km)	1,400 miles (2,300 km)	1,800 miles (2,900 km)	5 to 25 miles (8 to 40 km)
average temperature	up to 13,000°F (7,200°C)	8,000°F to 11,000°F (4,400°C to 6,100°C)	1,300°F to 7,000°F (700°C to 3,900°C)	up to 1,600°F (870°C)
made of	iron and nickel	mostly iron and nickel, possibly sulfur and oxygen	mostly silicon, oxygen, aluminum, magnesium, and iron	igneous, sedimentary, and metamorphic rocks

Volcanic eruptions, like this one, can be very beautiful. However, they're also very dangerous.

Igneous Rocks

The word "igneous" means "made out of fire." As magma is forced up to Earth's surface, it slowly begins to cool. As it cools, it creates igneous rocks. There are two types of igneous rocks—intrusive and extrusive.

Intrusive Rocks

Intrusive igneous rocks form when magma cools before it reaches Earth's surface. They're called "intrusive" because the magma has intruded, or been forced into, spaces between other rocks. In these spaces, the magma cools over a very long period of time, and this gives some of the minerals time to crystallize, or form crystals that are often large enough to see with the naked eye.

The most common type of intrusive igneous rock is granite. If you look closely at a piece of granite, you might see tiny pieces of minerals such

granite

as quartz, feldspar, and mica. Granite is a very useful type of rock. It's used to construct buildings and make tiles and other things you might find in your own home!

The kitchen countertop shown here
is made of granite.

Extrusive Rocks

Extrusive igneous rocks form on Earth's surface. They're called "extrusive" because the magma has extruded, or been forced out of Earth. Magma that pushes up through Earth's crust is called lava. Where lava flows out, it quickly cools and hardens. Over a period of time, the many layers of cooled lava form a **dome** shape. This is a volcano!

Because it's much cooler above ground than it is below, the lava cools more quickly, giving minerals less time to crystallize. The types of minerals in

the lava and the speed at which they cool decide what kind of extrusive igneous rocks will form.

Basalt is the most common extrusive rock in Earth's crust. The largest volcano in the world—Mauna Loa in Hawaii—formed almost entirely from basalt.

This vase is made of basalt.

Sedimentary Rocks

If you leave your favorite pair of shoes sitting outside for a long time, they'll begin to break down because of forces such as wind, rain, snow, and ice. If you leave them outside long enough, they'll fall apart. One day, you might find there's no trace of them left. The same thing happens to rocks! Eventually all rocks break into tiny bits of matter called sediment.

Sedimentary rocks form when a lot of sediment is pressed together in Earth. Just as there's more than one kind of igneous rock, there's more than

sedimentary rock

one kind of sedimentary rock. Scientists identify three types of sedimentary rocks: clastic, chemically formed, and **organically** formed rocks.

Clastic Rocks

Clastic sedimentary rocks are the most common type. "Clastic" comes from the Greek word *klastos*, which means "fragment" or "piece." Pebbles, clay, bits of rock, and sand—which are all forms of sediment—are carried by water, wind, or ice and in time settle somewhere else. This part of the rock cycle is called **deposition**. Heat, pressure, and minerals help hold these materials together. Over time, sediment forms solid rock.

Rivers carry a sediment called silt, which is deposited in larger bodies of water at the ends of rivers.

One kind of clastic rock is sandstone, which is formed over a long period of time by large deposits of windblown sand that become pressed together into a solid material. Sandstone is used mainly in the construction of buildings and home decorations.

sandstone

Chemically Formed Rocks

Chemically formed sedimentary rocks grow over a long period of time from minerals that have been **dissolved** in water. After the water **evaporates**, the minerals are left behind, creating a solid material. One of the most important types of chemically formed sedimentary rocks is called halite. You know this type of rock as salt!

Organically Formed Rocks

Organically formed sedimentary rocks grow from deposits of things that are organic, or were once alive. One common type of organically formed rock is limestone. Limestone is created when bits of shells and bones settle at the bottoms of oceans or lakes and, over time, solidify into rocks. In some pieces of limestone, you might actually see fossils of shells or tiny **organisms** that lived long ago.

This piece of limestone has a shell fossil in it.

Metamorphic Rocks

Metamorphic rocks are igneous or sedimentary rocks that change, or go through a metamorphosis, over a long period of time. These changes are caused by heat, pressure, or a combination of both.

Each type of igneous or sedimentary rock becomes a certain type of metamorphic rock. Take, for instance, the limestone that we discussed in the last chapter. Under the right heat and pressure, that limestone will one day turn into marble! Marble is a much harder material than limestone. It can be used in the construction of buildings. Some of the greatest artists in history, such as Michelangelo, used marble to create works of art. The Taj Mahal, considered to be one of the seven wonders of the modern world, is built out of pure white marble.

When granite is exposed to great heat and pressure, it can become a metamorphic rock called gneiss (NYS). This occurs commonly around the formation of mountains, where heat and pressure are very high.

gneiss

The Taj Mahal was completed in 1648. The Mughal Emperor Shah Jahan had it built as a tomb for his wife, who had died in 1631.

Instant Rocks

Most metamorphic rocks, like marble, develop over a long, long period of time, far beneath Earth's surface. However, some metamorphic rocks can form on Earth's surface in only a few moments. This occurs during a process called **shock metamorphism**.

When a rock from space falls to Earth, the crash can create high temperatures and pressure. In this situation, metamorphic rocks can form instantly. This can also occur if lightning strikes sand. The great heat of the lightning forms glass tubes called **fulgurite**.

fulgurite

Keep on Changing

After metamorphic rock forms, it can change again and become a completely different type of metamorphic rock. The sedimentary rock shale forms from clay that is packed together by great pressure. Under continued pressure, shale can turn into the metamorphic rock slate. If the pressure continues, this can cause mica crystals in the slate to grow larger, turning the slate into **phyllite**. More pressure will turn the phyllite into mica **schist**.

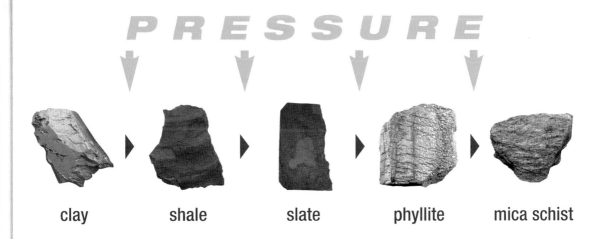

clay   shale   slate   phyllite   mica schist

Much of the island of Manhattan lies on top of a thick layer of mica schist. This layer, sometimes called Manhattan schist, forms a foundation for New York City's skyscrapers.

Even Earth Recycles

Now you know that rocks are always on the move. The rock cycle is called a "cycle" because there's no beginning or end to it. An igneous rock might eventually become a sedimentary rock or a metamorphic rock. A sedimentary rock can become an igneous rock or a metamorphic rock. A metamorphic rock might one day become an igneous rock, a sedimentary rock, or a completely different metamorphic rock. The process is never ending.

The rock cycle is important for keeping Earth's rocks in balance. If you think about it, Earth is actually recycling rocks, just as you might recycle an aluminum can or a newspaper! The only difference is that Earth's recycling process takes millions of years.

The energy produced inside Earth is what sets it apart from the moon or a planet like Mars. Neither of those places can support life like Earth

Scientists believe that the rock cycle will continue until the energy in Earth's core runs out. This could be another 4 to 5 billion years!

because there is no process that recycles materials they are made of. The rock cycle helps provide minerals to plants and animals that live on Earth.

The iron that you get from eating a big plate of spinach may have started out erupting from a volcano, cooling into a piece of basalt, breaking down over a long period of time, being carried by wind or water, and

eventually turning up in the soil where a spinach plant is growing. The plant takes the iron into its roots and one day might end up as part of your dinner. Iron is necessary to keep you healthy. Your body needs the minerals from Earth in order to survive. So, even if you aren't aware of it, you rely on the rock cycle every day.

The lava that erupts from a volcano cools to form basalt.

Over a long period of time, the basalt breaks down.

The basalt pieces are carried away by wind or water.

Basalt pieces end up in the soil.

A spinach plant grows in the soil.

The spinach plant takes in the mineral iron.

Our bodies take in the iron when we eat the spinach.

Seeing the Rock Cycle for Yourself

Most people can't visit a volcano to watch igneous rocks form or go to the bottom of the ocean to see sedimentary rocks in the making. However, there are many places to visit that can help you see and better understand the rock cycle. For example, you can see sedimentary and metamorphic rocks by visiting the Garden of the Gods in Colorado. There are ancient beds of shale, sandstone, limestone, and many other types of sedimentary rocks that formed millions of years ago but were forced upright by the formation of the Rocky Mountains. Heat and pressure from the uplift of the mountain formation created metamorphic rocks in the process!

Studying rocks and the rock cycle doesn't require anything more than a lot of rocks, a magnifying glass, and a notebook for writing about what you find. You can find rocks right in your neighborhood or just about any place you visit. It's challenging but very interesting and rewarding to study rocks and the rock cycle. It can help you gain a better understanding of how important rocks are to Earth and the future of our world.

Geologists think the rock formations in the Garden of the Gods began forming about 300 million years ago!

The Rock Cycle

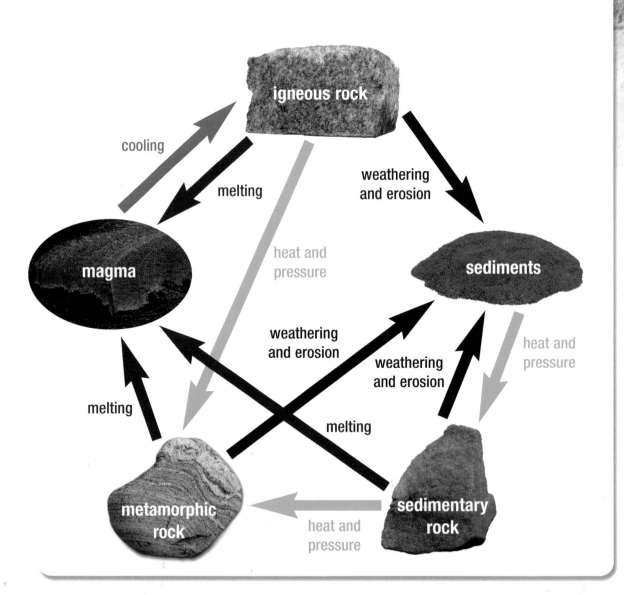

Glossary

cycle (SY-kuhl) A course of events that happens in the same order over and over.

deposition (deh-puh-ZIH-shun) The dropping of tiny bits of rock in a new place.

dissolve (dih-ZOLV) To break down and become part of a liquid mixture.

dome (DOHM) A type of curved roof or shape.

erosion (ih-ROH-zhun) The wearing away of land over time.

evaporate (ih-VA-puh-rayt) To change from a liquid to a gas.

fulgurite (FUHL-gyuh-ryt) A metamorphic rock that forms when lightning hits sand or rock.

magma (MAG-muh) A hot liquid rock underneath Earth's surface.

material (muh-TIHR-ee-uhl) What something is made of.

molten (MOHL-tuhn) Made liquid by heat.

organic (or-GA-nihk) Made from plants or animals.

organism (OR-guh-nih-zuhm) A living thing.

phyllite (FIH-lyt) A type of metamorphic rock.

schist (SHIHST) A metamorphic rock that can be split into layers.

shock metamorphism (SHAHK meh-tuh-MOR-fih-zuhm) The sudden formation of a rock from an extreme and sudden heat source.

Index